JOY, LIGHT, SORROW

JOY
LIGHT
SORROW
and
SPLENDOUR

Thoughts for our time
on the Rosary

CHRISTOPHER IRVEN

Brimstone Press

First published in 2007
by Brimstone Press
PO Box 114
Shaftesbury SP7 8XN

www.brimstonepress.co.uk

Designed by Linda Reed and Associates
Shaftesbury, Dorset, SP7 8NE
Tel: 01747 850487
Email: lindareedassoc@btconnect.com

Printed by J H Haynes and Co Ltd
Sparkford, Somerset, BA22 7JJ
Tel: 01963 440635
Email: bookproduction@haynes.co.uk

ISBN 978-1-906385-01-9

All images in this book, copyright
exemptions and the necessary permissions
from Private Collections, were obtained
and supplied by
The Bridgeman Art Library
17–19 Garway Road
London W2 4PH

The Annunciation, by Jacopo Tintoretto (1518–94),
Scuola Grande di San Rocco, Venice

From the bedlam of a violent world, and announced by Gabriel and a swarm of lesser angels, the Holy Spirit, the longing and self-giving of the triune God, finds refuge in Mary, his tranquil hiding place. God comes seeking the help of a young girl to set in train his plan to bring peace to the earth.

Contents

THE GLORIOUS MYSTERIES

Introduction

This is the most profound and searching series of meditations on the Rosary that I know. Chris Irven has found a point where the contemplative urge of prayer embraces an acute sense of suffering received and imposed, so as to focus the heart on its journey through the life of Jesus, a life lived and sacrificed 'once for all.' Time and again, in these meditations, you get an edge of meaning that touches and endures. It is not then surprising that this study takes in its stride the five newly added mysteries, called luminous, added by the last pope, and it had never struck me before that the traditional fifteen mysteries leave a gap, in the life of our Saviour, between the precocious twelve-year-old and the man of sorrows. Chris enables us to go across this vast gap with prayer.

Our age newly familiar with terror is also an age awakening to the Spirit, the love that casts out fear. We are experiencing birth-pangs of the Spirit such as Jesus in the fourth gospel foretold. The Spirit is now to be found in a way hitherto unknown, until René Girard discovered the victim at the heart of human history. I find this burning focus, of crucifixion seen through Easter eyes, in these wonderful meditations.

Sebastian Moore

Foreword

I am probably not alone in having found the rosary a difficult form of prayer. We know there are various ways in which it can be prayed. Some use it like a psalm, some as a mantra, constantly repeating the prayers as a soothing, time-marking background to meditating its mysteries. Others prefer to use the repetition to concentrate more and more deeply on the meaning of the words themselves. It can be a communal or private prayer, and if honest I have to admit that praying it aloud with others has never really worked for me.

Using it as a private meditation was not much better. The mental agility of saying one thing while thinking another was always beyond me. I became easily distracted, eventually running out of time and patience, having endlessly explored the red herringbones of my own thoughts. No doubt there is merit in persevering under difficulties, but it has one important drawback: a weak person gets fed up and drops it altogether. After several rather sporadic and half-hearted attempts to 'say' the rosary over a number of years in which I found it only dry and monotonous, the penny finally dropped: I needed a more structured framework for prayer. So I worked out a bead-by-bead discipline. To my surprise and delight it became alive for the first time, a maintainable habit. There may be many who have already found this out for themselves, of course, but it seemed only fair to pass these ideas on for those who have not. This book contains my bead-by-bead thoughts on the rosary as one example of this approach to the prayer.

On a practical point, an unhurried and thoughtful meditation of a decade's ten aspects, each marked by a bead, takes about fifteen minutes. Depending on the time available one might therefore decide to say either a five-mystery rosary lasting about an hour, or one or two decades as part of a daily routine of more general prayer. The aim, of course, is quality not quantity, and personal preference will decide. Perhaps the important thing is just to get on with it and leave Our Blessed Mother to teach the way best suited to each of her children.

In using any book such as this we should remember it is only an aid, much like a garden spade. The preparatory work starts with us. There comes a time when we put down the spade, get onto hands and knees and start planting tender shoots. God then takes over and makes them grow into things of beauty. What I mean is this: use the meditations in the book to help you imagine yourself actually present in the scene described. Remember Peter being questioned by those around the fire in the temple courtyard? Well, try to feel what he felt when Jesus glanced at him after he had denied knowing Jesus. Try to imagine our Lord's feelings! Or perhaps you could imagine being there at his birth, waiting with warm water and towels to wrap him in. Maybe *you* wrapped him up and gave him to his mother, stealing a quick kiss on the way. Maybe you kissed God… you would have done had you been there. If you are a young man, put yourself in the shoes of Simon the African. You are helping him to his feet, proud to be spat at and to carry the cross for a bit. Or again, at the end of this book, you might see yourself being carried up into heaven, welcomed by his mother and taken to her Son who reaches out to hold you fast.

One more tip: don't tie yourself down to a 'train timetable' (trains don't). If having embarked on, say, a decade you find yourself caught up and led into a deeper meditation than offered in the book, seize on it with delight. When Our Lord speaks, we drop everything and listen.

✢ ✢ ✢ ✢ ✢ ✢ ✢

The oft-repeated prayers of the rosary are the *Our Father*, the *Glory be*, and the *Hail Mary*. The first two will be found on the next page in the Introductory Prayers and will be well known by many readers. The *Hail Mary* is familiar to Catholics but may be less so to other readers, so has been printed below. It starts with the Archangel Gabriel's greeting when he visited Mary (the first decade of the rosary) and finishes with an intercession that she, God's mother, pray constantly for her disobedient children. Like the *Our Father*, it is best known in its Middle English form, and goes like this:

Hail Mary, full of grace! The Lord is with thee. Blessed art thou among women and blessed is the fruit of thy womb, Jesus. Holy Mary, mother of God, pray for us sinners now, and at the hour of our death. Amen.

Introductory prayers

The rosary has a 'tail' of beads from which hangs a crucifix. These are for introductory prayers and short meditations, such as the following.

The Crucifix. I believe in God the Father almighty, Creator of heaven and earth.

And in Jesus Christ his only Son, Our Lord, who was conceived by the Holy Spirit, born of the Virgin Mary, suffered under Pontius Pilate, was crucified, died and was buried. He descended to the dead and on the third day he rose again. He ascended into heaven and is seated at the right hand of God the Father Almighty, from thence he shall come to judge the living and the dead.

I believe in the Holy Spirit; the holy Catholic Church; the communion of saints; the forgiveness of sins; the resurrection of the body, and life everlasting.   Amen.

The first large bead. Our Father, who art in heaven, hallowed be thy name. Thy kingdom come. Thy will be done on earth, as it is in heaven. Give us this day our daily bread; and forgive us our trespasses as we forgive those who trespass against us. And lead us, not into temptation, but deliver us from evil.   Amen.

The three small beads, with thoughts on the Blessed Trinity and Mary.

1.   Hail Mary,
     Daughter of God the Father, the work of his hands, the pinnacle of all creation and our most highly favoured lady,
     Full of grace, the Lord is with thee! Blessed art thou among women, and blessed is the fruit of thy womb, Jesus. Holy Mary, mother of God, pray for us sinners now, and at the hour of our death.   Amen.

2. Hail Mary,

    Bride of God the Holy Spirit, his delight and sanctuary, the channel of all his graces,

    Full of grace, the Lord is with thee! Blessed art thou among women, and blessed is the fruit of thy womb, Jesus. Holy Mary, mother of God, pray for us sinners now, and at the hour of our death.   Amen.

3. Hail Mary,

    Mother of God the Son, in whose womb Existence Itself became enclosed that He might enter into given existence and be borne with a love beyond all telling,

    Full of grace, the Lord is with thee! Blessed art thou among women, and blessed is the fruit of thy womb, Jesus. Holy Mary, mother of God, pray for us sinners now, and at the hour of our death.   Amen.

The second large bead. Glory be to the Father, and to the Son, and to the Holy Spirit, as it was in the beginning, is now, and ever shall be, world without end.   Amen.

The *Joyful* Mysteries

✣

The Annunciation, by Dante Rossetti (1828–82), Private Collection

Tending the lilies in her fertile garden, Mary is startled by go-between Gabriel's request from God. Meanwhile the Holy Spirit hovers expectantly awaiting her reply. 'And the Spirit of God moved over the waters.' (*Gen 1:2*)

The Incarnation of Our Lord is announced

Dear Mother, teach us always to take God at his word, without interpretation to suit our own prejudice and preferences, but in perfect simplicity and trust for he cannot deceive.

Our Father…

1. The Word of God, only begotten Son of the Father, was given his human nature by the Father before time began. At the appointed time and place in history he was to take flesh, his kingly robe as the true and pre-eminent Adam, the ruler of all created things.

Hail Mary…

2. The Archangel Gabriel was sent to the Virgin Mary, the true Eve, to bring her the Good News. God stood cap in hand waiting for her consent to become the mother of the Word.

Hail Mary…

3. Mighty spirit though he was, Gabriel bowed low before this lowly handmaid of the Lord, this pinnacle of creation. 'Rejoice, most highly favoured Lady', he greeted her. Mary was astonished and alarmed at this greeting. 'Do not be afraid', he said, 'for you have found favour with God.'

Hail Mary…

4. 'Behold, you shall conceive and bear a son, and shall call his name Jesus' (which means God our Saviour).

Hail Mary…

5.   Mary accepted this simply and without interpretation but wondered how it would come about. 'How shall this be?' she asked, 'For I know not man.'

Hail Mary…

6.   'The power of God shall come upon you and the Spirit of the Most High shall overshadow you.' Then, filled with awe at the message he was bringing, he breathed, 'Therefore the Holy One that is born of you shall be called the Son of God.'

Hail Mary…

7.   Mary heard the angel's reply. She needed no further explanation or elaboration. She knew God's ways are not man's ways; God's thoughts are not man's thoughts. Unencumbered by the fearful reservations we call original sin, with utter simplicity and true humility in which there is no room for self-conscious false modesty she gave her answer: 'Behold the handmaid of the Lord. Be it done unto me according to your word.'

Hail Mary…

8.   Almighty God, and all heaven with him, breathed again. This perfect creature had exercised her freedom to its fullest potential, in complete harmony with Reality itself. We sinners can rejoice, for our salvation is assured.

Hail Mary…

9.   The bright seraph bowed low and withdrew from the presence of this exquisite vessel of God's grace, leaving her alone with God.

Hail Mary…

10. The Holy Spirit with ecstatic and boundless love possessed this most pure lady, and by his power she conceived, clothing in mortal flesh the Word of God. Our King fully shared our nature, becoming our brother and inseparable companion that he might feel first-hand all that we feel.

Hail Mary…

Glory be to the Father, and to the Son, and to the Holy Spirit, as it was in the beginning, is now and ever shall be, world without end. Amen.

*Mary in the House of Elizabeth (oil on canvas), by Robert Bell
(1863–1933), Private Collection*

Mary attends to her sewing while Elizabeth reads to her from a tiny book, the
two watched discreetly by Gabriel from the garden. The scene is cool and
serene, the two women in peaceful companionship while God is at work
within them.

✤ THE SECOND JOYFUL MYSTERY ✤
Mary visits Elizabeth and Zachary

Dear Mother, teach us to live in the present moment and to allocate our priorities according to the needs of others, leaving our needs to God's concern.

Our Father…

1. The Archangel Gabriel had told Mary that her cousin Elizabeth was expecting a child and was already in her sixth month. This was to show that with God all things are possible, for her husband Zachary was now old and she had always been pitied as barren.

Hail Mary…

2. Mary was at once filled with compassion for them both. Zachary had been struck dumb (for scoffing at the angel's message of the coming birth, though this would not be generally known), and Elizabeth, though overjoyed, would be feeling out of her depth and in need of someone to turn to.

Hail Mary…

3. So, forgetting her own momentous news and needs, Mary left at once for Zachary's house in the hill country of Judah, over a hundred miles away, her donkey led by the Archangel Gabriel as he had now taken her under his wing.

Hail Mary…

4. Having journeyed for nearly a week, they reached the house and Mary called out in greeting to Zachary and Elizabeth. They were all enfolded in the Holy Spirit.

Hail Mary…

5. Elizabeth, inspired by the Holy Spirit, cried out, 'How is it that the mother of my Lord should visit me? For when the voice of your greeting sounded in my ears the child in my womb leapt for joy. Yes, blessed is she who believed that the promise made her by the Lord would be fulfilled!'

Hail Mary…

6. Also filled with the same Spirit, Mary burst into her own paean of praise, 'My soul magnifies the Lord and my spirit has rejoiced in God my Saviour. He looks on his servant in her nothingness; henceforth all ages shall call me blessed. For he that is mighty has done great things to me, and holy is his name!'

Hail Mary…

7. Mary filled the house with laughter and mirth, a serious reverence but never a grave solemnity, for she was always such fun. Flowers seemed to be everywhere.

Hail Mary…

8. She helped Elizabeth prepare for the baby's arrival, inspiring the household with confident excitement. Tiny garments were knitted, a cot made ready. Occasionally Zachary would take his writing slate and slip out for a quiet stroll to catch up with old friends and escape the constant flow of girl-talk. Mary stayed the three months until the baby was born.

Hail Mary…

9. She witnessed the portentous signs surrounding the birth, how Zachary's tongue was loosed in praise and prophecy when he confirmed the child's name given him by the angel. A firm bond was established between the two families, from which would grow the close relationship between Jesus and John the Baptist, his precursor.

Hail Mary…

10. Her job done, Mary then returned to her own town Nazareth, nearly four months pregnant herself, to face the considerable misunderstandings and problems surrounding her own condition. She had dropped everything to attend to God's call upon her time: he would now look after her needs.

Hail Mary…

Glory be to the Father, and to the Son, and to the Holy Spirit, as it was in the beginning, is now and ever shall be, world without end. Amen.

The Birth of Our Lord Jesus Christ (gouache on paperboard), by James Tissot (1836–1902), Brooklyn Museum of Art

In wondering adoration, Mary worships the Fruit of her womb. Her cloak extends the protecting arms of a canopy above the tiny child whose radiance softly lights the rough-hewn birth chamber. Ox and ass join his mother in their own unblinking gaze at their Creator. His open arms betray the infinite self-giving love that has brought him to this place.

✥ THE THIRD JOYFUL MYSTERY ✥
The birth of Jesus

Jesus, Mary and Joseph, teach us to value poverty, for the poor know the true worth of things.

Our Father…

1. There being no room for him at the inn or in the homes of men, our Saviour and King was born in a cave. These ramshackle shelters afforded protection for some Bedouin families and their animals. Their inn crammed with travellers, the compassionate inn-keeper's wife had arranged this more intimate if smelly last resort for Joseph and his wife.

Hail Mary…

2. Calm and competent, and with the help of her daughter, this unchronicled wife of a poor Arab family delivered the Son of God to a waiting world. His blessed mother gave birth to him on her knees that she might be found worshipping him when he arrived.

Hail Mary…

3. The women picked him up and dried him, wrapped in his mother's shawl and gave him to her. She kissed him… and he, who knows all things, for the first time knew first-hand what it is to be loved as a human baby.

Hail Mary…

4. He cried and she cradled him to her breast. He remembered the security of the womb he had left, and sought consolation in the warm milk. And he, who completes all things, himself found completeness in one of his creatures.

Hail Mary…

5. Singing quietly to him, she swaddled his tiny sleeping form in her shawl and laid him in the springy hay of the manger. And he, who would be the food of all the world, lay in the eating rack of animals.

Hail Mary…

6. The ox and ass gazed on him and warmed him with their grass-scented breath. He would be the one through whom they and all creation would be drawn into the life of God, part of his story, the end of their groaning for completeness. And he, before whom the seraphim and cherubim veil their faces in heaven's endless day, rejoiced in the unblinking gaze of farm animals.

Hail Mary…

7. The angels who thronged the air in that holy place were astounded at this easy familiarity, this unselfconscious intimacy between God and his creatures. They burst forth upon the cold star-lit hillside where the shepherds were keeping their flocks and, filling the immensity of the night with their strange song, they said, 'Glory to God in the highest and peace on earth to men of good will. Come and see for yourselves what God has done for you!'

Hail Mary…

8. The shepherds went, led by the star, and found as the angels had said. They saw and they believed: no need for interpretation or plausible explanations. They fell on their knees before God-made-baby.

Hail Mary…

9. They offered him their gift, a new and perfect lamb, a living creature not made by the hand of man. For they were poor and knew the true worth of things.

Hail Mary…

10. Wise men too came from afar, our representatives bearing their credos in their gifts: gold, for he was king of all created things; incense, for he was true God of true God; myrrh, for he was truly mortal man.

Hail Mary…

Glory be to the Father, and to the Son, and to the Holy Spirit, as it was in the beginning, is now and ever shall be, world without end. Amen.

Flight into Egypt (oil on panel), Polish School (15th Century),
National Museum in Cracow

Enfolding him in their love and her cloak, Mary and Joseph bear their
precious charge on the donkey to present him to God in the temple in
Jerusalem a week after his birth. Less than two years later, the same donkey
and trio will flee to Egypt as a frightened King Herod murderously seeks to
destroy this imagined threat to his power, by slaughtering all baby boys in
and around Bethlehem.

✞ THE FOURTH JOYFUL MYSTERY ✞

Baby Jesus is presented in the temple

Dear Lord, teach us that whatever we give to you will be given back to us made nearer to perfection; and, which is infinitely more, you will give us yourself in return.

Our Father...

1. Obedient to the Jewish law, Joseph and Mary took Jesus to the temple in Jerusalem to consecrate their first-born son to God. As they were travellers far from home, he had been circumcised and named in the local synagogue when he was a week old, and they had stayed in Bethlehem another five weeks to be near Jerusalem when the time came to present him in the temple.

Hail Mary...

2. On that day they set out for the holy city, Mary riding on the donkey with Jesus inside her cloak, St Joseph leading; and the trio protected and guided by the Archangel Gabriel, while they rejoiced and thanked God for the blessing of their son.

Hail Mary...

3. They entered the gates of the City of Peace and went straight to the temple to pray and give thanks. Moved by the Holy Spirit, Anna the widow and prophetess who had served God for many years in prayer and fasting, came to meet them.

Hail Mary...

4. She recognised Jesus as the promised Messiah and gave thanks to God, and spoke of him to all who were looking for the deliverance of Israel.

Hail Mary...

5. Simeon, a devout man living in the city, had also been inspired by the Spirit to come to the temple that day. He recognized the baby as the Promised One, took him in his arms and thanked God: 'Now let your servant depart in peace, Lord, according to your promise. For I have seen with my own eyes the deliverance you have prepared for all peoples of the earth to see: a light to enlighten the gentiles and the glory of your people Israel.'

Hail Mary…

6. To the bewildered parents he said, 'This child shall be a sign of contradiction for the rise and fall of many, that the secrets of their hearts might be laid bare.' How true, for he would contradict all mankind's fearful and defiant denials of God's love throughout history in his resounding affirmation of God's will. And at the end of history it would be he who would judge the living and the dead.

Hail Mary…

7. Foretelling the deep sorrows she would bear as her share in the redemptive work of her son, he said to Mary, 'A sword shall pierce your heart.' She did not understand the prophecy, but would learn all too soon what his words held in store for her. In fear and rage at the foretold kingship of her child, Herod was to murder all male babies under two years old because of him, and the little family would be forced to flee into Egypt.

Hail Mary…

8. They offered Jesus to God, and in exchange for two doves, the offering of the poor, were given him back. What a barter that was: God Himself given to mankind in exchange for two tiny creatures!

Hail Mary…

9. So it is with us today. We give the Father the work of our hands, the fruit of the earth in the Mass, and in return he gives us his beloved Son to be with us and to be our food and our life.

Hail Mary…

10. And so it is in all our giving to God. We give him our hearts and our all, he returns them strengthened and cleansed. What starts as our presentation to God becomes his infinite presentation to us: an exchange of gifts between earth and heaven.

Hail Mary…

Glory be to the Father, and to the Son, and to the Holy Spirit, as it was in the befginning, is now and ever shall be, world without end. Amen.

Twelve-year-old Jesus in the Temple (pastel & gouache on paper), by Adolphe von Menzel (1815–1905), Hamburger Kunsthalle

Unabashed by the seniority and erudition of his listeners, the twelve-year old boy lays before them a wisdom of the Law and the Prophets that far exceeds even the excellent grounding learnt from his parents – who at that moment have happened upon the scene, relieved if exasperated. Attentive but astonished, the Jewish religious leaders listen to him, unaware that they are hearing the incarnate Word of God.

✛ THE FIFTH JOYFUL MYSTERY ✛

The child Jesus is found in the temple

Dearest Lord, let us start to learn that if we lose you we may always find you again by searching hopefully; and that having found you we must be about our Father's business.

Our Father…

1. When Jesus was twelve years old the holy family were on their way home to Nazareth in a caravan of friends and relations from their district, returning from the yearly Passover pilgrimage to Jerusalem. On the evening of the first day of their journey they met for the day's meal and found to their dismay that Jesus was not with them.

Hail Mary…

2. Each believing him to be with the other, Mary and Joseph had left him in Jerusalem. They were very worried, but it was too late to turn back that night so they committed all their anxiety to God and at last fell asleep for the night by the embers of the camp fire, the first day without him.

Hail Mary…

3. Early the next morning they awoke, untied the donkey, parted company from their friends who wished them good luck, and retraced their steps to Jerusalem under the guidance and protection of the Archangel Gabriel. That evening they reached the city and entered into its gates, finding a resting place for the night: the second day.

Hail Mary…

4. Foreshadowing the search of the holy women for their lost Lord on the day of his resurrection, Mary and Joseph rose early that third day and went to the temple to search for their child. And as on that Easter morning, Jesus was to be returned to those who sought him.

Hail Mary…

5. They found him sitting amongst the elders and scribes discussing the scriptures with them, listening to them and asking them questions. But to their astonishment, he was also answering their questions. All who heard him were amazed at the wisdom of a twelve year old boy, for how could they have known that he *is* Wisdom in person, the self-knowledge of the Father?

Hail Mary…

6. His mother said to him, 'Son, why have you done this to us? Your father and I have been searching for you in great anxiety.' And she could not keep the reproach from her voice.

Hail Mary…

7. His answer astonished them for it reminded them that he was more than just their son, that his mission lay far beyond the confines of their family. The Person of Christ, the Second of the Trinity, allowed a morsel of divine understanding to spill into the blossoming human intellect of this young boy. From a profound level of his dawning self-awareness, and in prophetic words which would be spoken later by his mother to him and finally by them both in unison, he said, 'Why did you search? Did you not know that I must be about my Father's business?'

Hail Mary…

8.	This answer, in its directness seeming almost like a rebuke, cut to the heart of Saint Joseph for he was reminded that he was not his natural father. Knowing this and loving him so dearly, Jesus then returned with them to Nazareth and was subject to them for eighteen more years. From then on only one tenth of his earthly days would be spent away from home. In the obscurity of his family and as the village carpenter, he would prepare himself for his public mission.

Hail Mary…

9.	He became the loving servant of his mother and the apprentice of his father-guardian, showing us family life in its perfection as he grew in wisdom and strength before God and men.

Hail Mary…

10.	We see the mystery of humility as the infinite God who made the unmeasured universe learnt the carpenter's trade at the hands of imperfect man.

Hail Mary…

Glory be to the Father, and to the Son, and to the Holy Spirit, as it was in the beginning, is now and ever shall be, world without end. Amen.

The *Luminous* Mysteries

✛

The Baptism of Christ (tempera on panel), by Guidoccio Cozzarelli (1450–1517), Pushkin Museum, Moscow

Meekly the unclothed Christ stands in the Jordan for cousin John's baptism, content to take upon himself and enter fully into mankind's fallen nature, that he might redeem it in his own person. As at his conception, the Spirit hovers like a dove upon him, indicating the divinity of the Son of Man.

✢ THE FIRST LUMINOUS MYSTERY ✢

The Baptism of Jesus in the Jordan

Jesus, when John baptised you in the Jordan you accepted the way marked out for you by the Father – to serve, to suffer and to die. Through our baptism give us the grace to follow not the world's way but yours.

Our Father…

1. The second of the epiphanies of Christ's divine and saving power was at the start of his public life. His reality hidden from all though increasingly seen by John, he mingled with the crowds of sinners he had come to save. At the end of his life's work, in shining glory and announced by his Father in identical words, he would be revealed to the chosen few on the mountain of his Transfiguration. But for now his glory lay hidden within his human frame.

Hail Mary…

2. The first reality manifested on Jordan's bank was that of the Trinity itself. Jesus is seen as equal to the Father and the Spirit. The meaning of Isaiah's prophecy is suddenly and unexpectedly made plain: *'This is my servant whom I strengthen, my chosen one in whom I am well pleased. I have filled him with my Spirit.'*

Hail Mary…

3. The presence of the Father is revealed to human ears. His voice is heard from heaven, 'This is my Son, the Beloved. Listen to him.' The primary relationship of the Trinity is opened to our understanding: when we hear the Son we hear the Father.

Hail Mary…

4. Immediately the second and third bonds of the Trinity are revealed to human eyes – the self-giving love of Father to Son and Son to Father. The Spirit is seen as a dove descending and alighting on the head of Jesus.

Hail Mary…

5. The manifestation of Christ's divinity is complete. The voice from heaven shows the Father's delight in him, the dove his Spirit conferred on him, and both point to the tangible presence of the incarnate Son of God pitching his tent among sinners.

Hail Mary…

6. Only John at once sees the fullness of this revelation and points him out to two of his own followers: 'Behold the Lamb of God! …He must increase and I decrease.'

Hail Mary…

7. John's water-baptism was given a new and lasting significance by this Spirit-baptism. From now on, baptism by water would become the symbol and sacrament of the waters of birth breaking onto the shore of a New Life, the means by which the Spirit would be conferred on us.

Hail Mary…

8. The second reality manifested that day in the Jordan was the acceptance by Jesus of his role of suffering servant. He took on our sins humbly and plunged into the waters, not because he needed to be cleansed but to signify the drowning of the sin of the world he would achieve. Later he would refer to his death as a baptism, and St Paul reminds us that 'in our baptism into Christ we were baptised into his death so that, dying with him, we might be raised to new life in his resurrection.' In taking the name Christian we follow our Master, pledging our lives for others even to death.

Hail Mary…

9.   In his baptism, Jesus prepared in his own person the re-birth meant for us. His credentials for doing so were impeccable for he is the true Adam and we are his descendants.

Hail Mary…

10.   After his baptism, the Spirit led him into the desert to prove his steel in temptation. Three times he was lured to abandon the daunting road to apparent failure and the grave that he had just accepted. In exchange, he could ease his hunger with a clear conscience and guarantee influence over those whose hearts he yearned to win – all for a perfunctory acknowledgement that evil could have its day as 'prince of this world', at least for the time being. As much despite his debilitating hunger and weakness as because of it, Jesus looked temptation squarely in the eye and then drove it from his presence.

O Lord, that we could do the same! Help us with your grace.

Hail Mary…

Glory be to the Father, and to the Son, and to the Holy Spirit, as it was in the beginning, is now and ever shall be, world without end. Amen.

The Marriage at Cana (oil on canvas), by Schnorr von Carolsfeld (1794–1872), Hamburger Kunsthalle

This stylised and idyllic depiction of the event shows six diminutive water jars rather than the barrel-sized stone containers the servants filled with water. Jesus directs and blesses while his mother keeps a low profile behind him. She has dropped a hint: it's now up to her Son. In the right background, constrained primly in their bower, the bride and groom must trust that their illustrious guest has everything under control and that not too many people will notice what is going on.

The marriage feast at Cana

Dear mother, you know how to plead for us to your Son better than anyone. Don't forget us.

Our Father...

1. For his third epiphany, Jesus chose a wonderfully human celebration – a marriage feast in a village near his hometown, called Cana. He and his mother had been invited, together with his friends.

Hail Mary...

2. He showed forth his divine glory by performing the miracle of changing water into wine. This was charged with symbolism. The water was held for the Jewish rite of purification in six huge stone jars. He had come to transform the old law into something joyous and delightful, water into fragrant wine; and what more perfect setting than a love feast, so symbolic of the banquet of the Lamb he had come to proclaim?

Hail Mary...

3. Towards the end of the feast, the demands of the well-oiled guests began to out-strip supply. His mother, with characteristic feminine alertness to matters practical and human, spotted the impending crisis. Sensing the growing anxiety of the bride and groom she felt sorry for them. She realized she would have to turn to her Son – an action in which she would later acquire great expertise, luckily for us.

Hail Mary...

4. So that the initiative for action might be wholly his, she would not ask him outright for 'a sign'. Instead, she would quietly draw his attention to the problem by dropping a gentle hint. 'They have no wine', she murmured. Would this not be her technique for drawing his attention to our plight when she sees her wayward children in a jam? Surely so!

Hail Mary…

5. 'Woman, why should that concern us? My hour has not yet come.' On the face of it his reply seemed detached, almost uncaring. Or was this the playful teasing by any son of his mother? If so, he had underestimated her: a Jewish mother needs no lessons on how to handle the good humour of a son enjoying the party. She would easily put the ball back in his court.

Hail Mary…

6. Besides, this hour, of the Father's choosing, was for his saving revelation. Mary did not press the matter. She well knew he would not allow the love feast to be spoiled by a slight miscalculation of how much wine was needed. Quietly to the servants she said (as she says to us) 'Just do whatever he tells you.'

Hail Mary…

7. As always, her instinct was right. Hour or no hour, Jesus was ruled by his heart. 'Fill the jars with water', he told the servants; and they did, all 150 gallons of it, enough for a thousand wine bottles in our measure! The prodigious generosity of God would always be his hallmark – in the wine at Cana, the loaves and fishes by the lakeside and the shoals of fish within it, or even his inexhaustible Body and Blood to feed the whole world.

Hail Mary…

8. Though the hour was for the Father's choosing, yet Jesus could do only what the Father did for he is the perfect image of the Father. So we can be sure that in seeing his heart moved by the embarrassment of the bride and groom, we see the compassion of our loving Father in heaven.

Hail Mary...

9. 'Draw some out now,' he said, 'and take it to the steward.' The perfection of the water-made-wine astounded the steward. The best had been kept till the last! We, the latter-day people of God, are the beneficiaries of his new dispensation that has turned the ritual water of the old law into the exhilarating and super-abundant wine of the new – his saving Blood.

Hail Mary...

10. His disciples, invited to the feast with him, saw this third manifestation of his glory, his first miracle, and they believed in him.

Hail Mary...

Glory be to the Father, and to the Son, and to the Holy Spirit, as it was in the beginning, is now and ever shall be, world without end. Amen.

The Miraculous Draught of Fish (watercolour & gouache on paperboard), by James Tissot (1836–1902), Brooklyn Museum of Art

While his friends struggle to land the gigantic catch oblivious of its source, Peter is more perceptive. 'Depart from me, Lord, for I am a sinful man', he says; but Jesus has other plans for them. 'Fear not,' he tells them, 'from henceforth you shall catch men'.

The proclamation of God's Kingdom

Jesus, you came not to condemn but to save. So, Lord, to whom shall we go? You have the message of eternal life.

Our Father…

1. Choosing Pan's own shrine at Caesarea Philippi as the battleground on which to declare the coming certainty of final victory, God turned hell's kingdom on its head. 'Who do people say the Son of Man is?' Jesus had asked his disciples and, amused, they gave their several replies. Then, seeing his seriousness they fell silent. 'But you,' he said, 'who do you say that I am?' Out of the silence the Holy Spirit spoke through Peter's dazed response, his words resounding from highest heaven through the waiting earth to the very mouth of quaking hell: 'You are the Christ, the Son of the living God!'

Hail Mary…

2. In faith we too acknowledge him as King of all created things in this world and the next. Day by day, and sometimes in our dreams, we listen for his call. Yet when he does, so often am I daunted by what he seems to be asking of me. Dare I leave behind all those vain things that charm me most? Like Simon, my sins ever before me, I am tempted to implore him to depart from me; but I must not. For he goes ahead of us the sheep of his pasture, and we follow because we know his voice.

Hail Mary…

3. What, then, is the kingdom of heaven – a pearl of great price or a hidden treasure worth all we possess? Perhaps we recognise it as the leaven quickening the whole dough, or the irresistible urge of the tiny seed to sprout and grow, we know not how. Or do we set our eyes on the banquet of the Lamb, the wedding feast of inexpressible love? Yes, all of these, but above all it is here and now. And more than that, heaven is within us if we only look!

Hail Mary…

4. Dear Shepherd-King whose voice I ache to hear, teach me how to make heaven in and around me. In childlike hope I trust in you, for only as a child can I gain heaven.

Hail Mary…

5. In hope I'll persevere, persist, pester like the importunate widow until my Judge hears my plea. In hope I'll stay awake, for so you have commanded me. And in hope I'll use the talents you entrusted to me, to delight you on your return.

Hail Mary…

6. For love of him I'll forgive even as I am forgiven. He is moved to pity when he sees me a long way off, waves aside my rehearsed speech when I sorrowfully return to him, places the best robe about my shoulders and sandals on my feet, and rejoicing leads me into the feast.

Hail Mary…

7. For love of him I will love myself that I may learn to love others for his sake. For his love I'll cherish all his creation, its wonder, beauty and laughter. I will listen for his voice in the animals, the wind, the sea and the silence of the stars.

Hail Mary…

8. For we are made from the dust of stars, as all earthly things are. And he too has hallowed our dust by making it his own, even to the cold tomb. Linked inextricably with him to all material creation and with our feet firmly in the clay, our eyes yet seek the very face of God.

Hail Mary…

9. Thus shall Alpha become Omega, his plan accomplished. Thus shall he draw all things in heaven and earth to himself, returning to the Father the primeval chaos made a new creation by his human touch.

Hail Mary…

10. And we shall proclaim his kingdom here on earth. We have worshiped him in the Gospels and in the Tabernacle: now we are to go out and find him in the oppressed and the despised and, falling on our knees before them, adore him there.

Hail Mary…

Glory be to the Father, and to the Son, and to the Holy Spirit, as it was in the beginning, is now and ever shall be, world without end. Amen.

Transfiguration of Christ (fresco), by Barna da Siena (~1350–55), Collegiata, San Gimigniano

The fresco conveys the dreamlike quality of the vision. For the three disciples, the constraints of time and space have shifted as in a waking trance. They recognize not only Jesus but also Moses and Elijah whom they have never met. The background, dark as night, accentuates the almost tangible hard edge of the halo, a brilliance that 'shone like lightning', for even before his death we are seeing the timeless reality of Christ's risen glory.

✛ THE FOURTH LUMINOUS MYSTERY ✛
The Transfiguration of Our Lord

Father, teach me each day to set aside some part from the pointless bustle of my life to be alone with you, that when at last I come fully into your presence I be not shy.

Our Father…

1. Jesus had rebuked Peter for remonstrating with him when he had warned them of his approaching suffering and death. He gathered the people and his disciples to him and told them that to follow him would mean taking up the cross. Then he foretold his transfiguration, saying: 'There are some standing here who will not taste death before they see the kingdom of God come with power.'

Hail Mary…

2. Six days later he took the chosen few, Peter, James and John up a high mountain to pray. Many times he had prayed like this to his Father, on mountains, in the desert, by the sea, beneath the stars. Often he had prayed with a group of his disciples or in the synagogue using psalms, prayers and scriptures. Now he would show his closest friends the first-hand experience of direct and lonely communication with God.

Hail Mary…

3. Compared to the first on Jordan's bank, this was to be a second theophany towards the end of his life's work, less public but more unmistakable. The experience would daze – almost stun – them; and they would not speak of it till after his resurrection. But it would strengthen them for the terrible days of betrayal, doubt and despair that lay ahead, tiding them over to that glorious culmination.

Hail Mary…

4.   While he became lost in prayer they watched him. The foundations of time and space seemed to move and their eyes grew heavy, as they would in that other mountain grove among the olive trees. But unlike that occasion, now they remained awake. They drifted into a higher level of consciousness, their eyes undazzled by the lightning brilliance surrounding them and the radiance of his countenance that shone like the sun.

Hail Mary…

5.   A shining cloud appeared and from it was heard the Father's voice: 'This is my Son, the One I love. Listen to him.' The greater the glory of the revelation, the more clearly is Christ seen in his proper context, the Blessed Trinity. Here as at his baptism, and in the very same words, he is revealed in his relationship to the Father, and within the bonding presence of the Spirit.

Hail Mary…

6.   But whence the nimbus surrounding Jesus? Throughout his life a realization had been growing within him of his oneness with God the Father. Now, this understanding had amounted to conviction, the physical impact on his body making it radiant. *

Hail Mary…

7.   But a shadow was cast too: this conviction had its dark side. This was no warm dream, no flight for Jesus from the horror that was to come. Rather, it was a preparation for it; for suddenly he was seen speaking to Moses and Elijah about *the passing he was to achieve in Jerusalem.'* Not just undergo, achieve. He knew his coming suffering and death was no imposition upon him from the Father but was to be his deliberate choice.

Hail Mary…

* *This understanding is attributed to Fr. Jerome Murphy-O'Connor, OP.*

8.   Peter, ever impulsive, ever full of childlike, unreasoning love, spoke from the depths of his dazed soul: 'Lord, it is wonderful for us to be here. If you wish, I will make three tents here, one for you, one for Moses and one for Elijah.' Dear Peter. Just say the word, Lord, and the job's as good as done!

Hail Mary…

9.   As if to emphasise the brilliance around them they were covered by shadow cast by the cloud. Overwhelmed by the numinous intensity of the vision and an overpowering sense of glory and melancholy, they fell on their faces in adoration, no longer daring to look up. Then they felt the gentle hand of Jesus on their heads and heard their beloved Shepherd's quiet voice. Looking up they were reassured: they were alone with Jesus once more.

Hail Mary…

10.   Dear Lord, when through your grace I find myself brought low into the awesome presence of our Father, reassure me, dear Brother, with your gentle touch and breeze-calm voice.

Hail Mary…

Glory be to the Father, and to the Son, and to the Holy Spirit, as it was in the beginning, is now and ever shall be, world without end. Amen.

*The Adoration of the Mystic Lamb – The Ghent Altarpiece
(oil on panel), by Jan van Eyck (1432), St Bavo Cathedral, Ghent*

The Banquet of the Lamb, of which the Eucharist is our foretaste.

'And I beheld a great multitude which no man could number, of all nations and tribes, and peoples and tongues, standing before the throne and in the sight of the Lamb, clothed in white robes with palms in their hands. And they cried with a loud voice saying: "Salvation to our God, who sitteth upon the throne, and to the Lamb." And all the angels stood surrounding the throne and the ancients, and the four living creatures, and they fell down upon their faces and adored God, saying: "Amen. Praise and glory, and wisdom, and thanksgiving, honour and power, and strength to our God for ever and ever. Amen." ' (Rev 7: 9-12)

✟ THE FIFTH LUMINOUS MYSTERY ✟
The institution of the Eucharist

O Jesus, this act of your enduring love and presence among and within us is a closeness transcending human love even at its most intimate, for you are to be our very food and drink!

Our Father...

1. For his last farewell supper with his friends before they would sit at table once more at the eternal banquet in heaven, Jesus chose the Jewish Passover meal of thanksgiving in which to institute the ritual feast of the New Law Christians would call the Eucharist. 'With longing I have longed to eat this Passover with you', he told them. Yet he spoke not just to his apostles that night but to us countless millions until the world's end. And he spoke with the longing, no less, of the bridegroom for his bride.

Hail Mary...

2. This was to be the celebration of the most intense, passionate and reckless love the world has ever known, the blueprint for every future act of human love, the master copy for his New Commandment to love one another as he has loved us. For love of us and that we might find peace he would place in our hands his life, his very self.

Hail Mary...

3. He taught his apostles this and how to exercise their leadership and authority through service, when he washed their feet. Peppery Peter fulminated at this supposed indignity of his Lord. Gently Jesus rebuked his protest and in good humour calmed his no less impetuous terror that he might find no part in him.

Hail Mary...

4. His mind went back to all he had done to prepare the people for this moment, perhaps the greatest moment since the creation of the world. He remembered the two occasions he had fed the bodies of the throngs following him, with loaves and fishes multiplied beyond counting, after he had fed their minds with his words. He remembered the synagogue in Capernaum where he had tried to coax the timid minds of his listeners to grasp what he was saying, so many of them drifting away when they heard him speak of his flesh as real food for their souls. Even now one of his chosen band would yet throw back in his face what he was offering. Would it all be in vain?

Hail Mary…

5. But now the die was cast; he had to go on in faith for this was what he had come to do. As he rent apart the great round loaf to share it with his friends he uttered the arresting words, 'This is my body.' He was speaking of the breaking of his body! He was speaking of his imminent death.

Hail Mary…

6. Moments later, the shared loving-cup of dark red wine eloquently confirmed the violence of his impending death. In no less disturbing words he told them that this was indeed how the cup of his blood, the New Covenant, would be poured out for all mankind for the forgiveness of sins. Solemnly they drank and passed the cup on.

Hail Mary…

7. To each he had given in its entirety his body and blood – his very self, undying. This literally true, it was his resurrected body because the resurrection would free him from the constraints of time and space. *'Then, immortal food supplying, gave Himself with his own hand'*, tells the Aquinas hymn.

Hail Mary…

8. One thing remained to do: this once-and-forever stupendous act of love-making had to be made accessible to time-bound humanity for always. This power of making his resurrected self present – anywhere in any age – had to be conferred upon his apostles. With divine authority and power he commanded: 'Do this in a making-present of me.'

Hail Mary…

9. From that moment they and their successors would have the irrevocable and terrible power to make him present to feed the flock he loved to death. From that moment he committed himself to be imprisoned in dark tabernacles throughout the world, waiting, waiting for the visits of his people for whom his heart longed. Never in all history had a man submitted himself to such loving bondage.

Hail Mary…

10. What have you done for us, Lord? You have blessed us with a sacrament for which all other sacraments were made, including mighty baptism itself. You have touched our space-time world with the timeless realm of God. So great that neither the cosmos nor heaven itself can contain you, yet you were pleased to rest as a seed within the Virgin's womb or a crumb within the cupped hand of the sinner! What can we say, Lord? Let your Mother (and ours) speak for us…

Hail Mary…

Glory be to the Father, and to the Son, and to the Holy Spirit, as it was in the beginning, is now and ever shall be, world without end. Amen.

The *Sorrowful* Mysteries

✠

Gethsemane, by Michael Ayrton (1921–75),
English © Private Collection/The Bridgeman Art Library

The Agony of Jesus seems to be shared and mirrored in contorted Nature
surrounding his bent and naked figure. His central position in the picture,
kneeling on a rock, calls to mind images of a victim upon an altar. All around
is death, decay and despair. Even the fallen tree in the foreground resembles
an obscene corpse lying in parched sand under a sinister smouldering
ambience.

✣ THE FIRST SORROWFUL MYSTERY ✣

His agony in the garden of Gethsemane

Loving and most forgiving Saviour, teach us to know how terrible sin is that we may avoid it with all our strength, for it crushed you nearly to death in the garden.

Our Father…

1. His act of self-giving at supper complete, Jesus knew he had handed over to his apostles absolute power over his body and blood. Even now that power was being betrayed into the hands of his enemies. He was filled with a sadness too profound for our emotionally stunted capacities to comprehend, not so much for fear of the consequences of that treachery as for the rejection of offered love.

Hail Mary…

2. Their last time together, he led his disciples out to pray in an act of loving trust to the Father's will. They descended into the Kedron Valley and up the other side to the Mount of Olives. As they climbed in silence, Jesus glanced to the left where the valley rose gently through gnarled trees. With a pang he realized that from one of those trees Judas would throw his life away in his final act of despair.

Hail Mary…

3. They entered through a gate into the olive grove known as Gethsemane. The day had been stifling but had now cleared, and the night air was heavy with the scent of growing things. Despite their protestations of loyalty, especially Peter's, Jesus had warned them they would all abandon him. He prayed that they be not permanently scattered but garnered and strengthened by the Spirit to face their own Calvaries.

Hail Mary…

4. Then, as on that day on the mountain of his transfiguration, he continued further up the hillside with Peter, James and John to the top of the garden where they could look across to the city. There was no moon that night – it would not rise for three days and indeed would blot out the sun itself the very next day – but the white houses and the temple shone coldly in the phosphorescence of the stars. He told them to wait there and stay awake while he withdrew a few yards. But soon they fell asleep and the stone's throw between them might have been a thousand miles.

Hail Mary…

5. He fell face to the ground in an agony of dread as he contemplated the suffering before him, leading to the step into nothingness that all of us must take in that final letting go. Twice he returned to his friends for a crumb of strength but found what all must find: death is the ultimate lonely act, and they were asleep.

Hail Mary…

6. Beyond his all-too-human dread of death he felt the terrible incompleteness of flawed human nature. For though he was its sinless head, yet it was a nature he shared. Its incompleteness, an affront to the perfection to which it is called, cried out to him for healing in a cry made deafening by its timeless concentration into one hour of one man's agony.

Hail Mary…

7. When things beyond our control go wrong we blame him. Is he not all-powerful? In a heartless existence we say he doesn't care: it's God's fault, God our scapegoat. The man-God knew that if we were to find healing he had to accept that blame – not for the evil we do for that would have been a lie, but for the resentment that wrenches our hearts. We had to pierce his heart. He prayed for another way to be found but there was none. An angel was sent to comfort him, and once again we see the astounding mystery of Almighty God being aided and strengthened by one of his creatures.

Hail Mary…

8. This was no sacrifice to a bloodthirsty Father, no pay-back for our rebellion. No, this was our hour, our time for God to pay, to be sacrificed for all our sufferings. And oh, how he yearned for our forgiveness! He returned again to his disciples and, finding them sleeping once more, wryly said, 'Sleep all you want now, it's all over, all too late. Look! Already they are at the gates.'

Hail Mary…

9. The temple guard came upon them armed with clubs and lanterns. 'Who are you looking for?' Jesus asked. They replied 'Jesus of Nazareth.' 'I am he,' he said. As Jesus himself had recognized when tempted on the pinnacle of the temple, throughout his life he would be protected by angels when his enemies would have destroyed him. Now this supernatural power threw his assailants to the ground. Once more he asked them whom they sought and this time, the supernatural guard restrained, they seized him. The disciples put up a dozy display of bluster and inaccurate swordsmanship before scattering like sheep as their shepherd was seized. One disciple, preferring to lose his cloak rather than his skin, evaded capture and ran naked into the night. How well I know the feeling, Lord!

Hail Mary…

10. Desolate, Peter followed his master at a safe distance before he too quailed under uncomfortably persistent interrogation, denied his master, and was brought close to despair by the glance Jesus turned on him. Then we see the preposterous spectacle unfolding of Justice Himself on trial by sinful man as he is dragged from one trumped-up court to the next.

Hail Mary…

Glory be to the Father, and to the Son, and to the Holy Spirit, as it was in the beginning, is now and ever shall be, world without end. Amen.

Christ at the Column (oil on canvas), by Georges Desvalliers (1861–1950), French © Musee du Prieure, Saint-Germain-en-Laye, France, Peter Willi/The Bridgeman Art Library

Overcome by the torture of the hundreds of cuts inflicted by the scourges, Jesus slumps unconscious. This will provide a short respite before a bucket of cold water is thrown over him to awaken him to the humiliation of his crowning with thorns and the horror of his journey to Calvary.

✟ THE SECOND SORROWFUL MYSTERY ✟
His scourging at the pillar

Dear Lord, by the agony you suffered in your scourging, teach us to calm our passions for you have borne our rage that we might find peace.

Our Father...

1. After an interminable night of insults and lies, the authorities could, of course, find no coherent case against him. But they were determined to have him killed anyway, so they handed him over to Pilate to do their dirty work for them.

Hail Mary...

2. Pilate knew Jesus had been handed over out of spite but he lacked the moral courage to acquit him. Besides, he had many pressing matters that day, and Jesus did seem something of a dreamer, lacking due respect for Roman authority. He therefore decided to hand him over to the soldiers to be roughed up a bit, while he had breakfast and considered what to do next.

Hail Mary...

3. The soldiers were going to enjoy this. This was a Jew and they hated Jews. They could beat this object up and feel better. They stripped it and bound it to a pillar, and gloated over its helplessness at their hands. Already they felt less afraid.

Hail Mary...

4. They beat it with whips of many leather thongs, each tipped with a dumb-bell of lead. The blows hissed down on back and legs and Jesus cried out in pain. His cries only increased their rage as they took it in turns to flog him.

Hail Mary...

5. The dumb-bells bit deep into his flesh and the blood ran down, laying bear his bones. But it is in his wounds that we are healed and in his blood that we are washed clean…

Hail Mary…

6. All this Jesus bore for us that we might be free from our anger and rage, and find peace from our restless passions.

Hail Mary…

7. In the end he began to drift into unconsciousness and the sport had gone out of it. Even though they took it in turns to whip him they grew tired and laid the whips aside.

Hail Mary…

8. They cut the cords binding his wrists to the pillar and he slumped to the ground unconscious. They revived him by throwing a bucket of water over him. The water washed the precious blood from his back and carried it into the drain in the courtyard to sanctify the very dust of the earth.

Hail Mary…

9. Pilate was still not ready to see Jesus, so they decided to add insult to injury. They sat him on a privy; 'a throne fit for the king of the Jews!' jeered some wag, and they laughed in his face.

Hail Mary…

10. Detesting all authority, about his shoulders they threw an officer's cloak, a kingly robe. In mocking this Jewish king, they could mock their own officers. Perhaps even now they might yet find relief from their bitterness.

Hail Mary…

Glory be to the Father, and to the Son, and to the Holy Spirit, as it was in the beginning, is now and ever shall be, world without end. Amen.

*The Crown of Thorns (watercolour & gouache on paperboard),
by James Tissot (1836–1902), Brooklyn Museum of Art*

Political turmoil between the Jews and their Roman overlords has been brewing for years and now threatens the social order called Pax Romana. Throughout human history, the solution to problems of this sort has been to direct the incipient violence on both sides against a common scapegoat. For this to work, the antagonists must convince themselves of the scapegoat's guilt: he, she or it (or they) is the cause of all their problems; and mockery and abuse are the tried and tested means of fanning up hatred which will make the subsequent murder of the scapegoat convincing and forgettable, a 'sacrifice', a making holy of the victim whose murder was therefore justified. This had always been religion's way. God's strategy of redemption for mankind is to allow his Son to become the victim and, through his rising from the dead and after that the work of the Holy Spirit, to convince the world of his innocence. This will finally demolish the founding lie of the scapegoat mechanism used by religions to preserve social order since time immemorial. Crowning Christ with thorns is this first necessary step in our redemption. We watch in pain and shame and gratitude.

✣ THE THIRD SORROWFUL MYSTERY ✣
His crowning with thorns

Dear Lord, by the humiliation and contempt you suffered at our hands, teach us from now on to see you in others and never to treat them with contempt.

Our Father…

1. 'A king needs a crown,' they said; and someone made a cap of cruel long thorns which they forced onto his head with rods. The thorns sank into his scalp, temples and forehead, and the blood ran down his face.

Hail Mary…

2. 'A king needs a sceptre,' they said; and they plucked a reed and stuck it between his bound hands. But the double irony was lost on them, for this sceptre was far more wonderful than any bauble made of gold and silver and precious stones by the hand of man. This was a living thing, a sceptre only God could make, fitting for the Lord of all created things, the Lord of life itself.

Hail Mary…

3. The king on his privy throne was ready for their homage. They spat in his face. They gestured obscenely to him. They bowed low and mocked him. And all these things they did *to Almighty God,* who held them in existence moment by moment. In our contempt of others – and ourselves – all these things we do to him.

Hail Mary…

4. They struck him in the face, and knowing he was blinded by spittle and bruises, by sweat and tears, and the blood running down his head, they asked him to prophesy who had struck him.

Hail Mary…

5. All this contempt he bore in silence, that we might be purged of contempt. Silently let me call to mind those my acceptance of an easy life consigns to poverty, degradation and contempt.

Hail Mary…

6. At last, Pilate was ready to receive him. They quickly took the officer's cloak from his shoulders and replaced it with his own garment. Then he was led into Pilate's presence by one of the guard. Secretly, Pilate was appalled at what the brutality of his men had achieved, but above all at what his own dereliction of duty had allowed to happen; and he looked for some excuse to release him.

Hail Mary…

7. Pilate looked on the terrible, silent dignity of the man, and instinctively recognised his majesty. 'Are you a king, then?' he asked. 'Your own words have said it,' Jesus replied, 'For this was I born, for this came I into the world.' Pilate felt the cold finger of fear touch the back of his neck. His wife's warning of foreboding in her dreams only increased his unease. From then on, he sought all the more earnestly to release Jesus.

Hail Mary…

8. 'Look at the man!' Pilate appealed to the crowd. 'Should I not release him to you?' 'No,' they howled, 'release us Jesus Barabbas.' A terrorist preferred to the Prince of Peace, a counterfeit man for the only ever true Man from the start.

Hail Mary…

9. 'What of Jesus Messiah?' Pilate pleaded. 'Crucify him!' they bayed, 'His blood be on our heads and on our children.' 'Shall I crucify your king?' Pilate whimpered. 'We have no king but Caesar,' they taunted him, and laughed mirthlessly at their political gibe.

Hail Mary…

10. In the end, for the sake of political expediency and 'in the public interest' Pilate abrogated justice and duty. Contemptuously consigning a man he knew to be innocent to a gibbet on the city's rubbish dump, in a ludicrously theatrical gesture he washed his hands. How little we have changed!

Hail Mary…

Glory be to the Father, and to the Son, and to the Holy Spirit, as it was in the beginning, is now and ever shall be, world without end. Amen.

On the Road to Calvary (oil on canvas), Dutch School (16th Century),
Private Collection, New York

In the hubbub of that awful journey there were four moments of relief, full
of the milk of human kindness: the meeting with his mother, the enlisting of
the support of Simon of Cyrene, Veronica's wiping his face with her veil, and
the sympathy of the weeping women. Three of the incidents involved the
compassion of women, just as all but one of his followers who stood by him
to the end were women. Here we see the courageous refusal of a woman to
be hustled along by the soldiers or the crowd. We can see in the face of Jesus
how much this sign of human compassion meant to him.

✛ THE FOURTH SORROWFUL MYSTERY ✛
The way of the Cross

Remind us, dearest Redeemer, that the cross you carry is our cross. We are the incomplete, the less than fully human. Give us the courage to share the load cheerfully for love of you.

Our Father…

1. They gave Jesus his cross. He accepted it with mixed feelings: feelings of dread for on it he would die a terrible death leading to oblivion; but also a certain defiant joy for by it he would save all mankind and give us a sign of his fathomless love which would last until the end of time.

Hail Mary…

2. So he embraced it and kissed it, and they didn't understand what he was doing. For God's ways are not man's ways and God's thoughts are not man's thoughts.

Hail Mary…

3. They laid the heavy gibbet on his shoulders and led him out between two thieves into the narrow streets crammed with the howling mob, the same crowd that only days before had cheered him to the echo as he rode in triumph into the city on a donkey.

Hail Mary…

4. Jesus stumbled and fell several times on that journey to his death, as we do. Each time he fought desperately to get up and continue, driven by a desperation to get the job done. Our loving Saviour was not dragged to Calvary; he struggled to get there.

Hail Mary…

5. Once he fell and thought he could not go on. All the world seemed against him. Then, there was his mother standing by him. He looked at her, seeking the help from that tower of strength that had never failed him in the past. She did not fail him now. She used the words she had long pondered in her heart, words he had used to her twenty-one years before when they found him in the temple. 'Did you not know,' she asked, 'that you must be about your Father's business?' She had *understood!* The poignancy surged through him and gave him renewed strength. He smiled, she helped him up, he hefted the cross onto his shoulders and continued on his way.

Hail Mary...

6. Another time, blinded by blood, sweat, spittle and tears, he stumbled. O if only I could have been there to help, for how we needed him to see his way to Calvary! Then, Veronica stepped forward on our behalf and wiped his face with her shawl. For this act of kindness to him and to us, he left the image of his face imprinted on it.

Hail Mary...

7. Once more he stumbled and this time he could not get up. Almighty God needed the help of frail man. The soldiers goaded and kicked him. Simon, a giant of a man, a stranger in the town, berated them for their brutality. Viciously they turned on him and constrained him to carry the cross. At first he protested: why should he get involved in this squalid Jewish Roman episode? Then he saw the appeal in the face of Jesus and suddenly he knew this was *his* cross this man was trying to carry! He waded in, roughly pushing the soldiers away and heaved the cross aside from where it was pressing Jesus to the ground. With the gentleness of controlled strength he helped Jesus to his feet. Then, with the cross laid on his own shoulders he said to Jesus, 'Come, my friend, we have work to do, you and I.'

Hail Mary...

8. On the way they met the weeping women, wailing in pity for him. But sorrowfully he remembered the cry of the crowd, 'His blood be on our heads and on our children.' 'Women of Jerusalem,' he said, 'weep not for me but for yourselves and for your children.'

Hail Mary…

9. At last they reached Calvary. With the ringing note of strong timber the heavy cross fell from Simon's shoulders and, with a last word of encouragement to Jesus, he fell back into the crowd. The soldiers stripped Jesus and while some fell silent at his gaunt and terrible beauty, others jeered.

Hail Mary…

10. They laid him on the cross, the altar of sacrifice, and stretched out his hands and feet, binding him to it that his arms might be extended in love to all mankind, even in death.

Hail Mary…

Glory be to the Father, and to the Son, and to the Holy Spirit, as it was in the beginning, is now and ever shall be, world without end. Amen.

The Raising of the Cross (panel), attributed to Peter Rubens (1577–1640), Musee Bonnat, Bayonne

Jesus, the ultimate scapegoat not just of man's fury towards God but also towards his fellow men, is finally bound and nailed to the Tree – paradoxically the Tree of Life – and raised up for all to see. There he will hang, an image of detestation and contempt like the bronze image of the fiery serpent raised up in Israel's camp in their journey through the desert. And just as those of Israel's tribe who were dying of snakebite lived if they looked upon the image on the pole, so would all people live who raised their eyes in trust to this latter-day image raised up to draw all men and women to himself.

✛ THE FIFTH SORROWFUL MYSTERY ✛

Jesus dies on the Cross

Dear Jesus, teach us to forgive all offences against us as you have forgiven us. My darling Saviour, where you have been I will gladly follow!

Our Father…

1. So desperate were we that he should not fall from the cross until the terrible sacrifice had been made that we nailed him to it, hands and feet. With clinical precision and an appalling lack of compassion, we drove the nails between the bones and into the hard wood. Jesus cried out to his Father to forgive us, for we did not know what we *are* doing.

Hail Mary…

2. Then the tree of life with its wondrous fruit, so long foretold and longer longed for in Eden's ancient myth, was raised up and planted in the hole prepared for it, heavy with fruit which must die and fall and go into the earth so that from it might spring everlasting life.

Hail Mary…

3. The crowd stood back and watched the agony creep over him. His followers for the most part stood afar off in despair, except for Mary Magdalene and St. John our representatives who stood at the foot of the cross with Mary his mother. Her mind went back to that little room and the great 'yes' she had given on behalf of all mankind. Now it had come to this, and Simeon's words rang in her ears. She *had* to hang on in trust. More than anything else he needed that now.

Hail Mary…

4. His enemies gloated and jeered. One of the thieves crucified with him tried to make light of it and said, 'Why don't you save yourself, Jesus? And us too while you're at it!' But the other thief bade him hold his tongue. 'We suffer as we deserve,' he said. 'This man has done no wrong.' Then turning to Jesus, with nothing to hope for except that Jesus might spare a passing thought for an old lag languishing in hell who had found a kind word to say for him, he added forlornly, 'Remember me, Lord, when you come into your kingdom.'

Hail Mary…

5. Here was unbounded joy indeed! Here was light at the end of the tunnel, something to make the whole ghastly thing worthwhile, his first customer. 'My son,' he said, 'this very day you shall be with me in paradise!'

Hail Mary…

6. 'I thirst,' he gasped. And well he might, for the brutality of his torturers had drained every drop of moisture from his body. But above all, he thirsted for our love, and all we had to offer him was the vinegar of our bitterness and gall. And even that he drank to the dregs that we might find peace.

Hail Mary…

7. He saw his mother and St. John at the foot of the cross and found a plan for the future dispensing of the fruits of salvation. He would give this wonderful mother to us too; he would hold nothing back. This was true Eve. 'Son, behold your mother,' he said, 'Woman, behold your son.'

Hail Mary…

8. He had given everything. A man can only die once, even though he would gladly have died for each of us in turn if he could. A man can only give the whole of himself. The great act of love, the greatest ever possible, had been consummated. 'It is accomplished,' he sighed.

Hail Mary…

9. He looked at last to his heavenly Father, and for a moment in that blissful face beyond suffering he saw a shadow of pain as the Father gazed on the awful incompleteness of human nature, the agony in his only beloved Son. Suddenly, in that terrible moment, our Saviour felt utterly alone, more alone than he had ever felt, a loneliness we can only glimpse at as we approach our own step into the nothingness of death. 'My God, my God, why have you forsaken me?' The sky turned dark and the earth shook as all creation recognised its own death in the coming death of its King.

Hail Mary...

10. The final moment had come: the great cry of affirmation cancelling out all the whimpering denials of men throughout history, the resounding 'Yes!' to the Father's will as God gave back to God his human spirit and with it all humanity, 'Father, into your hands I commend my spirit.' And bowing down his head, he died.

Hail Mary...

Glory be to the Father, and to the Son, and to the Holy Spirit, as it was in the beginning, is now and ever shall be, world without end. Amen.

The *Glorious* Mysteries

✢

The Resurrection (fresco), by Piero della Francesca (1420–92),
Pinacoteca, Sansepulchro, Italy

In the early light of dawn after the Sabbath rest, while the guards still sleep confident their dereliction of duty will go undiscovered, Christ awakes silently to everlasting life. The perspective of the trees converges, not on some infinitely distant vanishing point, but on an appearance here and now: not on Omega but on Alpha. 'Behold, I make all things new.' Triumphant over death, he carries the banner that henceforth will glorify the very sign of the instrument of his death. But this is no triumphal gloating over his victory: rather, a coming to terms with 'Sister Death' who will always be the gateway to unending life.

The Resurrection

Teach us, dear Lord, always to live in joyful hope of the everlasting life you have in store for us.

Our Father…

1. When Jesus died conquering sin and death he 'released the waiting dead' and descended into the abyss between this temporal world and the crystal-clear reality of heaven, filling even that dark recess of existence with his glory.

Hail Mary…

2. On the third day in the tomb, freed from constraints of time and space he rose to the full and complete reality of everlasting life.

Hail Mary…

3. He first shared his risen glory with his mourning but ever-trusting mother in a secret joy all their own.

Hail Mary…

4. Next, he appeared to Mary Magdalene in the garden. Foreseeing this moment, he had told her to keep the ointment she had brought him, until his burial. Now she came with it to say her last farewell, with James's mother Mary, and Salome; but they found the stone rolled back and the tomb empty. Heartbroken and blinded by her tears, most clearly she *saw* him – as the gardener, for so he was, the New Gardener in the New Eden! 'Sir,' she said, 'tell me where they have laid my Lord.' Laughing softly and tenderly at this darling, perplexed, muddled woman he uttered one word… 'Mary!'

Hail Mary…

5. She fell to her knees and wept for joy over his feet as she had wept for sorrow when first they met. 'Do not cling to my ankles,' he said, 'I must ascend to my Father! No, love me now with a far deeper, adoring love. I am your God.' So saying, he lifted her gently to her feet and solemnly they embraced.

Hail Mary…

6. Then Mary Magdalene ran as fast as she could to tell the others in the upper room. She burst in on their sombre silence, wild with joy. 'I have seen the Lord, he has risen!' Silly woman, they thought, always 'over the top'. But more kindly they said 'Sit down, Mary, calm yourself. Here, have something to eat and drink.' 'No,' she insisted, 'he *has* risen.' At the back of the crowd gathered round her, Peter and John exchanged glances. Was it just possible? Was this what he had meant? Hope began to stir, yet dared not utter itself. They slipped out without a word and ran to the tomb.

Hail Mary…

7. How they ran! Peter, his vision blurred with tears, kept repeating, 'Lord, let me glimpse you just one more time! Just long enough to say sorry, Lord!' John, the younger man, reached the tomb first but hesitated at the dark yet open entrance. Peter, impetuous as ever, came panting up behind and barged straight in. They saw the binding cloth, still wound round in a helix – but empty, limp, as if the body had passed straight through it, as if its physical power to constrain its contents had ceased to operate. They saw and they believed.

Hail Mary…

8. Jesus appeared to the disciples in the upper room. Suddenly he was there in their midst, through closed doors; but solid and utterly real. 'Peace be with you', he said; and then, as if he could not wait to hand on his new-won power of redemption to his instruments in the Church, he gave them the power to forgive sins. He also gave each of us the grace and power to forgive each other.

Hail Mary…

9. He appeared to two disciples on the road to Emmaus. At first they did not recognize him in his glorified state with all his reality simultaneously present. Their eyes as downcast as their spirits, Cleopas recounted to him the recent events that had dashed their hearts – though what the women had seen and heard had somehow kept their hopes a-smouldering. How strangely this stranger then replied, explaining the events in a light that had always been there yet never recognized! Then, in the evening they *knew* him in his gentle act of love, the breaking of bread. And they remembered how their hearts had burned within them.

Hail Mary…

10. Dear Lord, unlike Thomas I have not seen yet have believed. Strengthen my faith, bless me, let my heart burn within me, and bring me and all my loved ones to glorious resurrection into everlasting life.

Hail Mary…

Glory be to the Father, and to the Son, and to the Holy Spirit, as it was in the beginning, is now and ever shall be, world without end. Amen.

The Ascension (glazed terracotta), by Andrea Della Robbia
(1435–1526), Museo Nazionale del Bargello, Florence

Attended by the two angels who will send his little band of followers back to Jerusalem to await the coming of his Spirit in forty days' time, Jesus blesses them before being received from their sight for the last time on earth. Their eyes fixed on him, with aching hearts they see him go. But his command rings in their ears: 'When the Holy Spirit comes upon you, you will be filled with power, and you will be witnesses for me in Jerusalem, in all Judea and Samaria, and to the ends of the earth… and know that I am with you always to the end of time.' Though beyond their sight, they will never be alone. And their joy is ours, for the promise was made to us.

✙ THE SECOND GLORIOUS MYSTERY ✙
The Ascension of Jesus into heaven

Lord Jesus, our advocate pleading for us before the Father, teach us that if we die with you we shall also rise with you and be inseparable from you.

Our Father…

1. When his mission on earth was finished, Jesus gathered his mother and disciples to him and passed on to them the mission to spread the kingdom of God throughout the world. He led them out of the city to Bethany, raised his hands over them and blessed them.

Hail Mary…

2. He told them that all authority in heaven and on earth had been given to him, and with that same authority they were to go forth and teach all nations, baptising them and teaching them to observe all the things he had commanded them.

Hail Mary…

3. They would preach the gospel to all mankind, drive out demons in his name and bring hope and healing to a sad and hungry world. And through his self-giving – the Eucharist and the Holy Spirit – he promised to be with them always till the end of the world to strengthen them in their task.

Hail Mary…

4. Then they saw him lifted up, blessing them, until a cloud hid him from their sight.

Hail Mary…

5. They watched him go with mixed feelings, an aching sadness for they had been through so much together that it seemed their hearts would break, but also a triumphant joy for now they knew for certain what he was about.

Hail Mary…

6. While they stood there staring up into heaven two men in white, two angels, appeared to them. 'Men of Galilee,' they said, 'why are you standing there gazing up into heaven? You will see him return as you have seen him go. On your way now, for you have work to do.' And so they left in a spirit of resolve and purpose, returning to Jerusalem to await the coming of the Holy Spirit promised them.

Hail Mary…

7. Jesus was received into heaven with tumultuous joy and great glory, bearing his cross as the everlasting sign of his love and victory, and took his place at the right hand of the Father, resplendent in his human flesh: divinity, body and soul in-dwelt by the Holy Spirit.

Hail Mary…

8. In his arms he bears his own, those he has won through his cross. 'Father, in accepting my sacrifice you accept these who have shared it with me and who have washed themselves in my blood. I will never be separated from my little ones, bought at such great cost.'

Hail Mary…

9. In the mystery of seeing the sufferings of the Son, the Father is moved to infinite compassion. Thus in our Saviour's silent pleading is our salvation made effective.

Hail Mary…

10. The Father sees the Son and loves him boundlessly. In his human nature he sees all humanity for in Wisdom's blessed wisdom humanity must be shared, and all those who will not allow themselves to be separated from him are there. In this way we are drawn up into the very life of the Blessed Trinity.

Hail Mary...

Glory be to the Father, and to the Son, and to the Holy Spirit, as it was in the beginning, is now and ever shall be, world without end. Amen.

The Pentecost (oil on panel), by Fernando Gallego (1440–1507),
Iglesia de la Asuncion, Arsenillas, Spain

Suddenly the dark and cramped room in which they are sitting – more like a prison than a room – is filled with fiery light. Mary had been reading to the Apostles, but now their prayers are interrupted by a powerful wind blowing through the house and they are filled with God's presence. A new power surges through them, an urgency to spread the Good News throughout the world. For all except two of them (Mary and John), their zeal will lead to a martyr's death. But by then, the seed will have been sown. In only twenty centuries it will have become the greatest and most widespread religion the world has ever known, and will continue to grow until it embraces all mankind. Jesus said, 'When I am lifted up, I will draw all people to myself.'

✛ THE THIRD GLORIOUS MYSTERY ✛

The Holy Spirit comes on the fiftieth day

Holy Spirit, set us on fire with your life. Teach us to go fearlessly about God's business.

Our Father...

1. True to his promise at his ascension, on the fiftieth day after his resurrection Jesus sent the Holy Spirit to Mary and the apostles at Pentecost.

Hail Mary...

2. They were praying expectantly in the upper room in Jerusalem, barred and shuttered against the Jewish leaders who had had their master put to death, when suddenly the Spirit made his presence felt like the blowing of a mighty wind through the house, bursting open the shutters and letting in the light and air.

Hail Mary...

3. The very air crackled with electricity. Tongues of fire seemed to settle on the heads of each of them and they were filled with the Holy Spirit and an ardent love of God and all mankind.

Hail Mary...

4. They went out into the streets and Peter reminded the people of Joel's prophecy, *"'See, I shall pour out my Spirit on all flesh", says the Lord. "Your sons and daughters shall prophesy; your young men shall see visions and your old men shall dream dreams."'* Their fears and despondency vanished like morning mist on a summer's day, with Peter they all boldly preached the good news: 'This Jesus whom you crucified was the Son of God and has risen from the dead, and we are his witnesses.'

Hail Mary...

5.   The town was full of people from many different lands, yet each heard clearly in his own tongue the disciples' message as the Holy Spirit spoke directly into the heart of each of them. He who had dispersed men from Babel through a multiplicity of tongues that they might cover the face of the earth, now reunited them through a common understanding of God's word that Pentecost.

Hail Mary…

6.   Thousands repented and were baptised as the life-giving Breath of God blew where he willed.

Hail Mary…

7.   The new-born Church received her baptism that day and began her inexorable growth towards fulfilment when she will be ready for her Bridegroom on the Last Day.

Hail Mary…

8.   Holy Spirit, breathe life into our cold, dull souls. Replace our hearts of stone with hearts of flesh, burning with love of God and all mankind for his sake.

Hail Mary…

9.   Give us your sevenfold graces: wisdom that we may discern spirits; understanding that we may see God's will; counsel that we may spread his peace; fortitude that we may share his suffering; knowledge that we may know God even as we are known; reverence that we may honour him wherever he is to be found; awe that we may be filled with wonder at his presence in and around us.

Hail Mary…

✛ THE FOURTH GLORIOUS MYSTERY ✛
Mary is taken up into heaven

Dear mother, living proof, if proof were needed, of your Son's promise of our own bodily resurrection and ascension, pray for your straying children that we may come home to our inheritance.

Our Father…

1. Confronting paganism head-on as Jesus had done at Pan's shrine at Caesarea Philippi, God led Mary to the shrine of the goddess Diana at Ephesus after Jesus had ascended to heaven. It was there that St John took her, the mother of God, given to him and to us from the Cross, to a little house high in the hills above the town in Lydia, now western Turkey. There they lived in prayerful peace, Mary united to her Son in the Eucharist John ministered to her, visited from time to time by old friends and new converts as the Church spread outwards from its roots in Palestine.

Hail Mary…

2. When her life on earth was ended, she took her leave of John and was borne up body and soul to God in the arms of mighty Gabriel, her old friend. He carried her through the ranks of the heavenly host who parted and bowed low as she passed, and he laid her at the feet of God. This truth, imparted directly to the faithful by the Holy Spirit, was held and treasured by them for nineteen centuries before being declared an article of their faith by Peter's successor.

Hail Mary…

3. She was carried up body and soul, incorruptible in her resurrected glory, for she was perfect and corruption had no place or meaning in her.

Hail Mary…

4. She was carried up incorruptible for she was complete, perfect, as perfectly filling the limits set for her by God as her Son filled the limits set for his human nature by the Father.

Hail Mary…

5. She was welcomed by the Father as the pinnacle of his creation, as true an Eve as her son was the true Adam, and our most highly favoured Lady.

Hail Mary…

6. She was welcomed by the Spirit, for she is his delight, his bride, his hiding place, the vessel of his life and the channel of all his graces.

Hail Mary…

7. She was welcomed by the Son, and what a reunion that must have been as they fell into each other's arms never more to part! The angels watched in wonder as they had at our Saviour's birth, for here at the very heart of the Godhead, at the centre of Existence itself, was human embrace.

Hail Mary…

8. She was welcomed by the angels for she is their queen, the highest in the order of grace, with the moon beneath her feet.

Hail Mary…

9. She was welcomed by the saints, for it was through her consent to the Father's request that our Saviour was made flesh and salvation offered to all mankind.

Hail Mary…

10.   We too rejoice in the embrace of her and her Son, for like her we have arms to hold him and eyes to see him, and may hope to find ourselves drawn into the very life of God through his boundless love and his strong embrace.

Hail Mary…

Glory be to the Father, and to the Son, and to the Holy Spirit, as it was in the beginning, is now and ever shall be, world without end. Amen.

The Coronation of the Virgin (pencil, watercolour & bodycolour on paper), by Edward Burra (1905–76), English © Private Collection, photo © Lefevre Fine Art Ltd, London/The Bridgeman Art Library

She is our representative in heaven. We are her children and have a God-given first call on her time and care – every nation and creed under the sun, throughout history. She is our mother. She is Queen of angels, Queen of saints, crowned by the coarse workman's hands of her strong Galilean Son, who is also King of earth and heaven. Neither she nor her Son is an easy pushover, for they love us with the wide-awake love of those who know all too well what it is to be human. And they will never abandon us in all our joys and sadness and weaknesses. So all of us whoever we are – fishermen, women in the home or streets or market place, men in trade or teaching or fighting, conversing or arguing, living, loving or dying – we can all trumpet the news of her crowning. It's an exultation taken up by the angels themselves for she is their honour as much as our boast. So, strum the guitars and let the horns blow!

✠ THE FIFTH GLORIOUS MYSTERY ✠

Our Lady, Queen of angels and saints

Be always with us, dear mother, to remind us that our business is to spread God's kingdom on earth as it is in heaven.

Our Father…

1. Mary was crowned in heaven, Queen of all the angels and saints, by the hand of her Son, King of all created things.

Hail Mary…

2. She was crowned for her simplicity, her acceptance of God's will at face value without interpretation, diminishment, adjustment or condition.

Hail Mary…

3. She was crowned for her great wisdom for she is the Seat of Wisdom. She accepted God's word, then pondered it in her heart and made it her own.

Hail Mary…

4. She was crowned with great rejoicing in heaven. But we too join our voices with theirs as we say:

Hail Mary…

5. Above the rejoicing in heaven she hears the distant pleading of her feeble children, and at her command heaven falls silent and listens.

Hail Mary…

6.   She turns to her Son and he smiles, for this was his plan on that dark day on Calvary when he gave her to us and us to her.

Hail Mary…

7.   They look at each other and spontaneously they say together those words first used by him to her in the temple, and then by her to him on his way to Calvary, 'Did we not know that we must be about our Father's business?'

Hail Mary…

8.   Together they laugh, for this had always been his plan. He knew first-hand her strength when he had felt down and out, and had wanted that strength to be at our disposal too. So, merrily their laughter fills all heaven.

Hail Mary…

9.   Heaven takes up their mirth and rings with joy, for he has done all things well.

Hail Mary…

10.   We too can laugh and be merry, for she will never abandon her children on their journey. And as she is now our strength and our hope so one day she will be our Queen too.

Hail Mary…

Glory be to the Father, and to the Son, and to the Holy Spirit, as it was in the beginning, is now and ever shall be, world without end. Amen.

Closing prayer

At the end of the rosary prayers, one, five or more decades or whatever is chosen, we may conclude with one of the great prayers of the Church to our Blessed Lady, just to wrap things up. Some of these are suggested here.

Remember, most loving Virgin Mary, that it is a thing unheard of, that anyone fled to your protection, implored your help or sought your intercession, and was left forsaken. Filled therefore with confidence in your goodness I fly to you, Virgin of virgins, my mother. To you I come, before you I stand, a sorrowful sinner. Despise not my words, O Mother of the Word, but graciously hear and grant my prayer.   Amen.

Hail, holy Queen, mother of mercy, hail our life, our sweetness and our hope. To thee do we cry, poor banished children of Eve. To thee do we send up our sighs, mourning and weeping in this vale of tears. Turn then, most gracious advocate, thine eyes of mercy towards us, and after this, our exile, show unto us the blessed fruit of thy womb, Jesus. O clement, O loving, O sweet Virgin Mary!

Mother of Christ, hear your people's cry,
Star of the Sea and Portal of the Sky.
Sinking we strive and call to you for aid,
Mother of him who you from nothing made.
O by that joy which Gabriel brought to you,
You Virgin first and last, to us your mercy show.